CONTENTS

OOH, IT'S DARK IN HERE.

POLICE

LIGHTEN UP, SUNSHINE!

WE ARE NOT AMUSED!

1ST

NOT-FOR-PARENTS

GREAT BRITAIN
Everything you ever wanted to know

I THINK I'D LOOK BETTER ON A BATSMAN THAN A BOWLER.

THIS IS MY LUCKY SHIRT.

I DON'T LIKE THIS HAT, BUT I'M GOING TO BITE MY LIP.

I'M FEELING A BIT DIZZY.

NOT-FOR-PARENTS

THIS IS NOT A GUIDEBOOK. And it is definitely Not-for-parents.

IT IS THE REAL, INSIDE STORY about one of the world's most exciting places – Great Britain. In this book you'll read fascinating tales about **kids down the mines**, battles on the football field, **secret stones** and kings and queens galore.

Check out cool stories about a famous spy, an **underwater monster**, a **flying scotsman** and a flying great grandmother. You'll find hats and bats, **crazy laws**, royal limos and some amazing **legends**.

This book shows you a **GREAT BRITAIN** your parents probably don't even know about.

A GREAT LAND

Great Britain is the name given to the island that is made up of three great places with three great names: England, Scotland and Wales. The great land of Great Britain has a great many great names. There are old names, long names, rude names and just plain silly names.

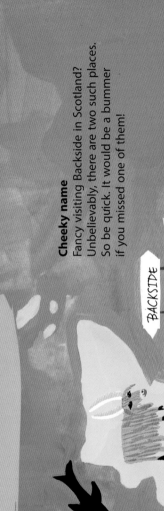

Scotland

Cheeky name
Fancy visiting Backside in Scotland? Unbelievably, there are two such places. So be quick. It would be a bummer if you missed one of them!

Windy name
Scotland can be windy, and it might be slightly more windy in the town of Brokenwind in Aberdeenshire!

Lost name
You are not likely to get lost in the tiny village of Lost in Aberdeenshire. However, there is one thing that keeps getting lost – its road sign. Some tourists find it a great souvenir.

Noisy name

If you head to Great Snoring in Norfolk, it might pay to take some earplugs. If the noise gets too much, Little Snoring might be quieter.

GREAT SNORING

HAM

GRAVESEND

Food name

One place in Kent could make you hungry. The town of Sandwich is near a hamlet called Ham. A famous sign that points to the hamlet and town reads 'Ham Sandwich'!

CRACKPOT

SILLY LANE

MOLD

England

SCRATCHY BOTTOM

Wales

LLANFAIRPWLLGWYNGYLLGOGERYCHWYRNDROBWLLLLANTYSILIOGOGOGOCH

Grave name

Some towns are good to live in when you get older. You can bet that Gravesend in Kent will make a good final resting spot.

Village name

There is a village in North Yorkshire known as Crackpot. It is not named after some eccentric English person, but rather a crack in a rock.

Old name

With a name like Mold, this market town in North Wales has definitely seen its fair share of mouldy vegetables! The town sprouted up around Mold Castle in the 1100s.

Street name

Some road names in Great Britain make you laugh. Funnily, Ha-Ha Road in Greenwich is nowhere near Silly Lane in Lancaster.

Long name

The longest place name in Great Britain is Llanfairpwllgwyngyllgogerychwyrndrobwllllantysiliogogogoch, which means 'the church of St Mary in the hollow of white hazel trees near the rapid whirlpool by St Tysilio's church of the red cave'. Whew! Just call it Llanfairpwll for short.

Funny name

You would probably not stop smiling if you lived in Happy Bottom in Dorset. Mind you, Scratchy Bottom in Dorset might be funnier!

WANT MORE?

BRITISH BULLDOGS

Some say that the British love their dogs more than they love their children. That might be a bit of an exaggeration, but many pet owners definitely treat their dogs like royalty. Even the royal family's pet pooches are treated like kings and queens!

BULLDOGS DON'T HAVE A STIFF UPPER LIP!

A miniature poodle

The leader of the pack
During World War II, the great leader Winston Churchill was nicknamed 'the British Bulldog' by the Russians because of his fierce fighting spirit. If only they had known that his dog was a poodle.

Bulldog buddy
The British bulldog was first used to guard and bait bulls and bears from the 1200s until the 'sport' of bull baiting was banned in 1835. Today, pet bulldogs are more likely to guard their food bowls!

AND BUDDIES

Pet power

King Charles II was besotted with his dogs to the point that he made a decree that the King Charles spaniel could go in any public place and even in the Houses of Parliament. This law still stands today.

I DON'T THINK DOGS LOOK LIKE THEIR OWNERS.

King Charles II

Not King Charles II

LOYAL TO THE ROYALS

Dogs can be a queen or king's best friend. Queen Elizabeth II is a loyal corgi owner. She has had pet corgis for more than 79 years!

In 1910 King Edward VII's fox terrier, Caesar, was loyal to the very end. He walked in procession behind his master's coffin.

A corgi

A fox terrier

I LOOK LIKE THE DOG'S DINNER IN THIS SCARF.

Pubs and pooches

Many pubs welcome dogs (and their owners!). Some serve dog-friendly pub grub. One pub dishes up Sunday roast with cat-flavoured gravy made from beef stock and fish sauce! It can all be washed down with a cool non-alcoholic dog beer.

WANT MORE?

Find out more about dog breeds. www.the-kennel-club.org.uk

QUEEN OF HEARTS

Mary, Queen of Scots was a bit of a drama queen. At just six days old, she became Queen of Scotland when her father, King James V, pegged it. She later hooked up with a succession of hopeless husbands during her reign. Unlucky in life *and* unlucky in love?

> IS SHE DEAD GORGEOUS OR GORGEOUS DEAD?

Teen queen

In 1558, aged 15, Mary married the young crown prince of France. By the age of 17, she was a widow. Her husband had died of an illness brought on by an ear infection, which ended up destroying much of his brain!

KISSING COUSINS

In July 1565 Mary married her cousin, Lord Darnley. Mr Right turned into Mr Wrong. Darnley was a selfish man, who some believed wanted Mary dead.

A killer of a crush

Mary soon detested Darnley and grew to fancy the Earl of Bothwell, who ended up murdering Darnley in February 1567. Mary wasn't too upset. She played golf just days later.

Loved by a loony

French poet Pierre de Boscotel de Châtelard wanted to be Mary's suitor but ended up being her stalker. On 14 February 1562, he hid under her bed. His obsession with her eventually got him hanged.

> YOU ARE MY VALENTINE!

I WONDER WHO IS GOING TO WEAR THE PANTS?

Escaping Lochleven Castle

'I'd love to help'
In July 1567 Mary was forced to abdicate and was imprisoned in Lochleven Castle. Luckily, a lovesick man nicknamed 'pretty Geordie' helped her escape the next year.

Mary's third husband, the Earl of Bothwell, kidnapped her and forced her to marry him!

Lord Darnley and Mary, Queen of Scots

Loyal to a royal
Mary had a very loyal subject – her dog. After being imprisoned for 19 years by Queen Elizabeth I of England, Mary was beheaded on 8 February 1587. Her dog hid under her dress!

WANT MORE?

Mary was a half-sister of Elizabeth I ☆ **www.royal.gov.uk**

ARISTOCRATIC ECCENTRICS

The fifth Marquess of Anglesey was slightly bonkers. It wasn't so much his pink poodle or the perfumed exhaust on his car that gave it away, it was his over-the-top obsession with gorgeous gems and jewel-encrusted costumes. Great Britain has had its fair share of aristocratic eccentrics who were without a doubt definitely a few diamonds short of a necklace!

I'M A REAL GEM.

Loony lord
Lord Berners was bonkers about colours. He dyed his doves pastel colours and ate colour-coordinated food. If the Lord fancied a red lunch, he would be served tomatoes, strawberries, lobster and beetroot soup!

The fifth Marquess of Anglesey

Eccentric earl

Every night, a dozen dogs dined with the eighth Earl of Bridgewater. They dressed for dinner, wore leather boots and had linen napkins. Each dog had its own footman. Those paw men!

STOP DROOLING. HERE COMES YOUR SAUSAGE, DOGS.

The second Baron of Rokeby floated for hours in water.

Screwball squire

The Squire of Halston Hall, 'Mad' Jack Mytton, might be the maddest aristocrat of all. To cure his hiccups, he set himself alight. The last thing he hollered before he died was, 'Well, the hiccups is gone.'

Crazy countess

The Countess of Cardigan and Lancaster liked to dress as a nun or a Spanish dancer at the dinner table. She also kept a coffin in her hallway, and a number of times a day, her servant would lift her into it so that she could try it out for size.

Demented duke

The fifth Duke of Portland was a recluse. To avoid talking to people, he had two letter boxes in his bedroom: one for incoming mail and one for outgoing. His doctor had to stand outside his room while a servant took his pulse.

I'M SURE THERE WAS MORE LEG ROOM THIS MORNING.

WANT MORE?

Police were called 'Peelers' or 'Bobbies' after their founder, Sir Robert Peel.

BOBBIES IN BLUE

Sir Robert Peel started up the London Metropolitan Police Force in 1829. Pretty soon the streets swarmed with police with their eyes peeled for pickpockets and prowlers. The police were not popular, even with the public. Dressed in top hats and long, blue tailcoats, the constables were supposed to look more like citizens than soldiers. But they weren't all law-abiding – out of the first 2800 recruits, 2328 were dismissed for breaking the rules!

DOCTOR WHO? NO ONE HERE BY THAT NAME.

THAT'S A WEE PROBLEM.

A pee-wee crime
It is against the law to urinate in a public place – or is it? A pregnant woman can wee into a police officer's helmet!

Call the police
Blue police boxes were once familiar sights on street corners. Police used them to phone the police station.

Coppers and cars

The police are often called the 'Old Bill'. One story about how the nickname came about is that some police cars used to be registered with the letters BYL. How about this for a police number plate – URBUSTD.

KID CRIMES

The Metropolitan Police Act of 1839 has laws that are still in place today. Children are forbidden to:

☆ slide on ice or snow or fly a kite
☆ set off fireworks or build bonfires
☆ ring a doorbell (without permission)
☆ bait a bear!

To raise the alarm, the police used to have wooden rattles!

Police HQ

Newsflash! Scotland Yard is not in Scotland. It is the headquarters of the London Metropolitan Police. It got its name because its original building was used to house important visitors from Scotland.

A ripping case

Between 1888 and 1891 the police in London were not just trying to apprehend robbers, they were after a ripper, too – Jack the Ripper, who got the nickname because he ripped open his female victims to remove their organs. Suspects included a school teacher, a thief and a quack-doctor. You could say Jack the Ripper got away with murder. He was never found.

I WAS NEVER CAUGHT RED-HANDED!

Body in the basement

On 2 October 1888 a copycat killer put a cat among the pigeons. Police found a female torso in the cellars of Scotland Yard's new headquarters, which were being built in Whitehall. A sniffer dog located the victim's left leg near the building site!

WANT MORE?

Metropolitan Police official site ☆ **www.met.police.uk**

A shot Scot
If you are Scottish, you would certainly want to know what day of the week it was if you were visiting York in England. It is still legal to shoot a Scottish person with a bow and arrow, except on Sundays.

THE MAN'S GOING TO GET US KILLED!

PUT ME UPSIDE DOWN AND YOU'LL BE IN JAIL LICKETY-SPLIT!

LAUGHABLE LAWS

Have you ever licked a stamp with the Queen's head on it and then plonked it upside down on an envelope without thinking? Well, think again! You're breaking the law. In fact, that offence is treason, which was once punishable by death. Luckily today, treason will just get you life in prison. There are many laughable laws from long ago that still exist in England, but if you are from Wales or Scotland, don't think you've got off scot-free, because some of the laws affect you – and they are no laughing matter!

LAWS OF PARLIAMENT

★ It is illegal for MPs to wear armour in the Houses of Parliament, and has been since 1313. Guess that was an unlucky year!

★ It is best not to die in Parliament. It's not against the law, but the Palace of Westminster is a royal palace. So technically, if you die there, you need a state funeral.

A burning problem

Long ago in England, people practising witchcraft were punished by hanging, but in Scotland, they were burned instead. It gets worse. They had to pay for the fuel for the fire!

I'M SMART. I BROUGHT MY OWN FUEL!

Danger in the dark

If you are a Welshman visiting Chester in England, don't think that you'll get to do a spot of sightseeing at night. Welshmen cannot enter the city before sunrise or stay after sunset!

Eating mince pies on Christmas Day is against the law!

I'M JUST PLAYING DEAD.

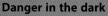

RANDOM RULES

★ It is against the law to impersonate a Chelsea Pensioner – a former British Army member.

★ In St Peters, women cannot show their ankles in public.

★ In London, taxi drivers cannot carry dead bodies or rabid dogs.

★ In Kidderminster, you cannot own a bath without a watertight plug.

WANT MORE?

A London taxi driver is meant to ask passengers if they have the plague!

COOL CANALS

In the 18th century, Great Britain went canal crazy, with watery motorways criss-crossing the countryside. Plenty of people lived, worked and even went to school on canals. Some families lived on one-bedroom canal boats. Boat life was hard, and children had to grow up fast. Many were lent or even sold to other boats to make way for new siblings!

CANAL KIDS

These kids at their canal-side classroom were lucky – most boat people never stayed in one place long enough to learn to read and write.

The workers who dug canals were called 'navvies' (from 'navigator').

Going underground
When the canals went underground, it was time to leg it! 'Legging' was the art of pushing a canal through a tunnel with your legs. Some tunnels were up to 5km (3mi) long – that's an awful lot of legwork!

YOU PUT YOUR LEFT LEG IN, YOU TAKE YOUR LEFT LEG OUT...

LYING DOWN ON THE JOB AGAIN, I SEE!

IT'S SAFER IF I WALK BEHIND.

Canal killer
Living and working on canal boats could be dangerous. Drowning was a common cause of death. George Summers probably thought he was safe riding slowly on his canal-boat horse along the tow path beside the canal. That is, until his head hit a low bridge and he was killed!

Canal boats were long and skinny to squeeze through tight spots on canals.

I MIGHT JUST LEG IT THROUGH THIS WINDOW.

Don't look down
With a 38m (125ft) drop just centimetres away, this aqueduct in Wales is the tallest and scariest canal crossing in the world. Superstitious builders added ox blood to the mortar for good luck!

CANAL ROBBERS

Some canal people had a terrible reputation as thieves. In 1838 some boatmen were caught stealing £600 worth of silk (that's more than £55,000 in today's money!). They soon found themselves on a different kind of boat – a convict ship bound for Australia!

WANT MORE?

SECRETS OF THE STONES

The Stone Age people who made Stonehenge didn't believe in doing things the easy way. They lugged some of the heavy stones 250km (155mi) from a hillside in Wales. Stonehenge's mighty stones were aligned with the position of the sun at midwinter and midsummer. But the discovery of human remains there suggests it was more than just an oversized observatory!

WHO ARE YOU CALLING AN ANCIENT MONUMENT?

Midsummer madness

Every midsummer, modern-day witches and druids dust off their robes and head to Stonehenge for a pagan party. Stonehenge has a special meaning for many people. Some connect it with ancient religions. Others claim it is proof that we have been visited by UFOs!

STONE STATS

- ✷ Equal to 540 adults – weight of the heaviest stone
- ✷ 33m (108ft) – diameter of outer circle
- ✷ 250km (155mi) – distance to Preseli Mountains in Wales, where some stones were quarried
- ✷ 3100 BC – first earthworks built on site
- ✷ 1600 BC – last stones put in place
- ✷ £6600 – sum Cecil Chubb paid to buy Stonehenge in 1915. He gave it to the nation three years later.

Dead and buried

The grisliest Stonehenge secrets are the remains of injured or disabled people. Some experts think they prove that Stonehenge was an ancient healing centre. Others reckon it may partly have been a fancy cemetery – with unusually big gravestones!

I'M A HEAD OF MY TIME!

Stonehenge means 'stone gallows' in Old English. Gallows were used for hanging people.

Well-travelled stones

Nobody really knows how these huge stones were transported from Wales. Some people think they were carried as far as possible by boat, then dragged overland on timber rollers and finally hoisted into position.

MAYBE A GIANT DOMINO SET?

Silbury Hill near Stonehenge

Unnatural feature

The plain on which Stonehenge stands is littered with other prehistoric monuments. One of the weirdest is Silbury Hill. It is an artificial hill as big as an Egyptian pyramid and about as old. When archaeologists tunnelled inside, they found 4500-year-old grass so well preserved that it was still green!

WANT MORE?

Stonehenge ✷ www.stonehenge.co.uk

SPOT THAT LOCO

Trains are a great British invention that made a great British hobby possible – trainspotting. The aim of a trainspotter is to see (or 'spot') every example of a type of locomotive or carriage. When a train is spotted, the trainspotter writes the details in a notebook or takes a photograph. Exciting, or what?

The Flying Scotsman
This loco used to run from London to Edinburgh non-stop in under eight hours. You can spot it on special outings.

WINCHCOMBE

I'VE GOT A ONE TRACK MIND.

The Mallard
In 1938 this machine ran at 203km/h (126mph), a world record for a steam locomotive that still stands today. You can spot the Mallard at the National Railway Museum in York.

The Mallard

L N E R 4468 MALLARD

The Flying Scotsman

I'M PASSENGER SPOTTING.

Eurostar Class 373

You'll have be quick to spot this locomotive. It goes at over 300km/h (185mph). It's the best way to get from London to Paris.

Eurostar Class 373

DO THE LOCOMOTION

Does trainspotting sound like fun to you? No? Then maybe you'd be interested in one of these related hobbies.

Haulage bashing
This is a bit like trainspotting, but you must note down the details of the locomotive then catch a ride in a carriage behind it.

Line bashing
This is the attempt to travel an entire railway network: every station, every curve and every straight.

Timetable collecting
That's right. Collect as many timetables as you can, new and old. Some people like to collect train tickets too.

The current record for passing through all 270 stations of the London Underground is 16 hours, 29 minutes and 57 seconds.

Stephenson's Rocket

The Rocket was the first locomotive to haul a regular passenger rail service. You can spot it at the Science Museum in London.

The Rocket

WANT MORE?

National Railway Museum ★ www.nrm.org.uk

Free for all
Once football was a game
you made up as you went
along. You could even pick
up the ball and invent rugby!
(See pages 60–1).

ON THE BALL

The British have enjoyed playing football for centuries
but before 1863 every club, school and village played by
different rules, which made playing a match far from home
almost impossible. Finally, the Football Association was
formed and everyone agreed on the rules. Now football
is the most popular sport in the world.

Meet you in the pub

The Football Association was formed in a series of meetings in London's Freemasons Arms pub in 1863. Twelve teams were involved – most of them long since extinct.

I'M HAVING A CRACKER OF A GAME!

Almost half a billion people watch the FA Cup final on television.

GIANT KILLERS

The Football Association runs the annual FA Cup. Over 700 clubs compete, from giants like Chelsea and Liverpool, to village teams. In 2008 amateur team Chasetown became the lowest-ranked team ever to reach the third round of the FA Cup. Then they played (and lost 3–1) against Cardiff City, a team six levels and 135 places higher up.

FA Cup trophy

Shin kicking okay?

One team quit the negotiations in disgust because they wanted it to be legal to kick your opponents in the shins. The other teams thought this was a bad idea.

WANT MORE?

www.thefa.com/TheFA/WhoWeAre/HistoryOfTheFA

UPSTAIRS, DOWNSTAIRS

Imagine having to be invisible and face the wall if you met your employer on the stairs. Servants long ago were divided into those who were allowed up the stairs and those who never dared venture near them. Servants usually slaved away for about 16 hours a day. Sunday afternoon was their only time of rest.

> I'M ALLOWED UP THESE STAIRS. I HAVE TO CLEAN THEM!

STAIR STATUS

The servants allowed 'upstairs' included the butler, housekeeper, footman, nanny, lady's maid and valet. The servants confined to 'downstairs' included the laundry maid, kitchen maid, scullery maid and hall boy.

Cunning cooks

In the days before fridges, keeping the food fresh was a full-time job. Luckily, cooks had many tricks to bring dodgy food back to life, like stuffing a whiffy chicken with charcoal to absorb the odours of decay!

The hall helper

Servants were general dogsbodies, and their accommodation was usually cramped quarters in the attic. The hall boy's digs – on a fold-down bed in the hallway – might seem spacious in comparison.

Chamber chores

A chambermaid's chores were like the chamber of horrors! People used to urinate or deposit their 'night soil' into chamber pots, which they kept under their beds. Chambermaids were kept a wee bit busy, cleaning the 'gazunder' pots four times a day.

THIS BUSINESS MAKES ME POTTY!

In the 1600s servants used to sleep in the same bedroom as their employers!

Busy butlers

Butlers were the vital link between the upstairs and downstairs. Their work was varied, from inspecting servants' fingernails to ironing their boss's newspapers to remove the smell of ink or the trace of newsprint!

WANT MORE?

Some grand houses had tunnels so that the servants could not be seen.

THE SEA CLOCK

The British rightfully used to boast that 'Britannia rules the waves.' But Captain Cook and co owed their seafaring success to one unlikely figure: a self-taught clockmaker named John Harrison. Before him, a ship at sea had no way of knowing its longitude – that is, exactly how far east or west it was. A wrong guess could, and often did, spell total disaster!

That sinking feeling
In 1707 four British ships and more than 1400 men were lost when the fleet collided with the Isles of Scilly. A rich prize was offered for a solution to the 'longitude problem'.

LONGI-WHAT?

The lines of longitude go from pole to pole. To work out your longitude, you just need to compare the time where you are with the time at Greenwich, in London. But in the 18th century there were no clocks that would keep the right time on a rocking ship!

John Harrison

Nutty notion
One plan for keeping time at sea involved putting a wounded dog on every ship. At the same time each day, someone back on shore would dip one of the dog's old bandages into a magic powder, called Powder of Sympathy. Supposedly, the poor pooch on the other side of the world would instantly whimper, letting the ship's captain know the exact time!

OUCH! IT'S TIME THEY FOUND A BETTER WAY!

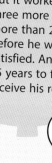

Longi-dude
When John Harrison heard of the £20,000 prize being offered by the Board of Longitude, he set to work building a reliable sea-going clock.

YOU'RE WINDING ME UP!

Harrison's first sea clock

Time machine
Harrison's first clock looked more like an alien spaceship than a clock – but it worked! It took three more clocks and more than 20 years before he was totally satisfied. And another 15 years to finally receive his reward!

EVERY STORY NEEDS A VILLAIN!

Nevil Maskelyne

Royal pain
The Astronomer Royal, Nevil Maskelyne, wasn't impressed by Harrison's ticking toys. He thought the longitude problem could only be solved by astronomy. He did all he could to stop Harrison getting his hands on the prize, even seizing Harrison's clocks and plans.

WANT MORE?

Captain Cook called Harrison's clock his 'faithful guide' ☆ www.rmg.co.uk/harrison

A RING OF CASTLES

King Edward of England was a bit of a bully who ruled with an iron fist. By 1283, after conquering Wales, he set about building a ring of castles in North Wales known as the 'iron ring'. His castles were like a ring of steel, but Welsh rebels didn't let towers, moats and murder holes stop them from trying to win back Wales.

The fabulous four

Four castles make up the 'iron ring': Caernarfon, Conwy, Beaumaris and Harlech.

Caernarfon Castle

WELSH CASTLE WORDS

afon – river

bryn – hill

caer – fort

carreg – stone

castell – castle

clwyd – gate

dinas – fort

hen – old

llys – court or hall

Built to last?

The castles in the 'iron ring' did not always keep people out. In 1294 the Welsh prince Madoc took advantage of an unfinished wall in Caernarfon Castle. He and his supporters temporarily captured the castle and set much of the timber alight.

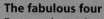

Beaumaris Castle

WHAT IF THEY BUILD A BOAT?

Mighty moat

Beaumaris Castle never got a chance to see battle during Edward I's reign. Its 5.5m (18ft) wide moat stopped people in their tracks. Its 'murder holes', through which people in the castle could pour boiling oil or water onto those below, might have put off any would-be attackers, too.

Harlech Castle

HELP, HELP...

River defence

Conwy River almost helped Prince Madoc when it flooded in 1294. It meant the English soldiers could not help Edward, who was in Conwy Castle, at least not until the river subsided. During the siege, King Edward was not impressed. He had to eat peasant food!

Conwy Castle

IT'S A VIEW TO DIE FOR!

Castle on a crag

Prince Madoc was busy in 1294. He tried to seize Harlech Castle, which sits on a rocky crag, but he didn't manage to succeed. Soon King Edward had an idea. He imprisoned Scottish rebels there. After all, who could rescue them?

There are more than 400 castles in Wales.

WANT MORE?

FLAMING HOT

Curry – some like it hot and some like it not!
Great Britain was never famous for food that
set your tastebuds on fire. But when people
from places such as India and Pakistan settled
there, they brought with them curry recipes
that packed a punch. Now people throughout
Great Britain love their curries, and even have
chicken tikka sandwiches for lunch!

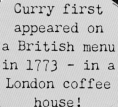

ROAST CURRY, ANYONE?

Curry first appeared on a British menu in 1773 – in a London coffee house!

Roasted curry
British people love their roasts. In the 1800s, during the British rule of India, the Indian cooks had to do something with all the leftover cold roast beef and potatoes. The result was a sizzling new dish – jalfrezi.

Eat the heat
An exceptionally hot curry, phall, was invented in Great Britain. One chef, who claims to make the world's hottest phall, wears a gas mask when he cooks it.

Spice of life
Ginger is a tangy spice used in some curries. In the 1500s King Henry VIII believed that this spice would protect his people from the plague. It didn't.

About 50,000 curries are eaten in Scotland every night!

By the bucketful
In Birmingham in the 1970s, factory workers needed a curry in a hurry. Pakistani restaurants whipped up balti, which was cooked and served in a metal, wok-like pot. The pot is called a balti, which means 'bucket'.

BECOME A CURRY EXPERT

If you don't know your aloo from your elbow, now's the time to start learning. Match each word to its meaning:

naan

jalfrezi

tandoor

kulfi

lassi

aloo

A: a popular dish cooked with onions and peppers

B: potato

C: a delicious Indian ice cream

D: a chilled yoghurt drink

E: a clay charcoal burning oven which is used for baking

F: a thick, flat bread made with special flour, yeast, eggs, milk and sugar

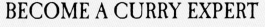

Answers: naan=F; jalfrezi=A; tandoor=E; kulfi=C; lassi=D; aloo=B

Chips and curry
In the 1950s, in the aftermath of World War II, some Bangladeshi seamen bought up bombed-out fish and chip shops in the East End of London. They soon offered a new kind of topping for the chips – curry sauce, of course!

I SHOULD BE SAFE IF I FLY TO BOMBAY.

Duck out of luck
Fancy some duck curry? Well, you would be out of luck if you ordered Bombay duck. That dish is made of salted sundried fish.

WANT MORE?

The Curry House ✕ www.curryhouse.co.uk

THE TREASURE KEEPERS

DO I REALLY NEED 23,000 COINS AND MEDALS? YES!

Imagine filling your house up with so many old bones, treasures, mummies, coins, fossils and specimens in jars that you needed to buy the house next door to make room for your ever-expanding collection. That's what happened to Sir Hans Sloane, part-time collector and full-time hoarder. He poured all his spare cash into a colossal collection that grew so big and impressive that he bequeathed it to King George III in 1753. Six years later, in 1759, the British Museum started up and has been the keeper of Sloane's treasures ever since.

Sir Hans Sloane

Peculiar paintings

Collectors look for unusual pieces. Sloane was no different. He must have been thrilled when he found a landscape painting done on a spider's web.

By the time Sloane died, he had collected more than 71,000 objects.

Skull of a rhinoceros hornbill

GLAD THIS ISN'T A TWO-HEADED DINOSAUR.

THAT'S WEIRD!

Sloane's collection of bizarre objects included:

- ✰ stones from the bladders of horses
- ✰ hairballs from the stomachs of cows
- ✰ ground mummies' fingers
- ✰ archers' rings
- ✰ a skull of a rhinoceros hornbill (that's a bird)
- ✰ a glove knitted from the silky filaments made by a type of large mussel

Interior of the British Museum

Housing the treasures

When Sloane died, the government went house-hunting for new premises. They were keen on Buckingham House (aka Buckingham Palace), but it was rejected as too pricey and not a great location!

Up in smoke

The actions of the early 1800s might have seen Sloane turn in his grave. The natural history keepers did a clear out of 'zoological rubbish', and soon the neighbours complained of the smell of burning snakes.

I'VE COME TO SEE THE ASTROLABE.

I WANT TO SEE THE HAIRBALLS.

Sloane also collected scientific instruments – but he was more interested in their looks!

Dusty old collections

One man who helped keep Sloane's collection clean was Henry Hook, who held a Victoria Cross for bravery. He was the 'inside duster' of the sculptures for many years until he was promoted to looking after people's umbrellas!

WANT MORE?

Astrolabe, for locating planets and stars

The British Museum official site ☆ www.britishmuseum.org

WHAT THE DICKENS?

Life could be grim for children in the 19th century. Some were packed off to brutal schools. Others were put to work for a pittance. When superstar author and all-round celebrity Charles Dickens was young, he had been forced to work in a filthy factory. He never forgot the experience and used his stories to shine a light into the darkest corners of Victorian Britain.

I'VE GOT MY EYE ON YOU.

Wackford Squeers
(*Nicholas Nickleby*, **1839**)

Cruel school
Dickens based his cruel, one-eyed schoolmaster, Wackford Squeers, on a real Yorkshire schoolmaster named William Shaw. Shaw had to shut down his school after his pupils began going blind.

DICKENS LANE

Charles Dickens

YOU BETTER WATCH WHERE YOU'RE GOING!

Caught short
The heroine of *Little Dorrit* grows up inside Marshalsea debtor's prison. Dickens knew the prison well – when he was 12, his family ended up there after his father was arrested for debt. Charles was packed off to work in a boot-polish factory.

Clean sweep
In the days of horse-drawn coaches, a crossing sweeper would clear a path through the poo on the street. Jo, a crossing sweeper in *Bleak House*, was said to be based on 14-year-old George Ruby, who was called to testify in court.

Jo the crossing sweeper
(*Bleak House*, **1853**)

Little Dorrit
(*Little Dorrit*, **1857**)

CRIME KIDS

Pickpockets, such as *Oliver Twist's* Artful Dodger, could be sentenced to hard labour. Sometimes this just meant turning a crank in their cell all day. The crank could be screwed tighter by the prison warders – which is where they got the nickname 'screws'.

BET THERE'S A TWIST TO THIS STORY...

IT COST ME NOTHING TO BE IN THE DICTIONARY.

Mean geezer
Some wealthy Victorians built schools, houses and hospitals for the poor. Dickens took aim at the other kind when he created mean old Ebenezer Scrooge. Scrooge is so miserly, his name has entered the dictionary meaning a 'tight-fisted person'.

Ebenezer Scrooge
(*A Christmas Carol*, **1843**)

WANT MORE?

The genius of Dickens ☆ www.charlesdickenspage.com

COAL AND KIDS

In the 1700s coal made Great Britain a superpower, but it also made many of the kids just exhausted. Back then, children had some of the weariest, dreariest jobs around. Imagine what it must have been like for the poor Scottish girls who had to cart coal on their backs up steep ladders. Coal and kids helped make Great Britain truly great, but it was certainly not a time to be claustrophobic, afraid of the dark or scared of heights!

MINING'S THE PITS.

WHEN I GROW UP, I WANT TO BE A MINER LIKE MY DAD.

DANGER ZONE

Often whole families worked in the mines. Mining accidents in Wales frequently killed hundreds of miners:

☆ 439 killed at the Universal Colliery at Senghenydd on 14 October 1913
☆ 290 killed at the Albion Colliery at Cilfynydd on 23 June 1894

Children sorting coal, Wales

Children spent up to 14 hours a day down the mine, but there were no toilets.

CLEANING COAL

Long ago, coal heated many people's homes, which gave rise to another job for children – a chimney sweep.

The age of misery
In 1842 Parliament passed a law banning all underground work for women and girls and for boys under the age of 10.

I'D RATHER BE A SHIRKER THAN A WORKER.

Feet and fire
Climbing up a chimney flue was scary work. To get reluctant chimney sweeps to climb up, older boys were sent up behind them to stick pins in their feet or to brush their feet with burning straw!

Naked truth
Soot would often fall into the pockets of the chimney sweeps, which could cause them to become stuck in the flue. To stop that, chimney sweeps often worked naked.

SHUT YOUR TRAP!

I FEEL TRAPPED.

Draggin' a wagon
'Hurriers' did that – hurry. These kid couriers hauled coal wagons through damp, cramped corridors. The girls and boys were often almost bald from pushing the wagons with their heads.

Trapped in the job
'Trappers' sat alone in the dark. They had to open a trapdoor for the hurriers. In 1873 one trapper who fell asleep on the job had his leg cut off by a coal wagon!

WANT MORE?

The Industrial Revolution began in Great Britain.

TEA MANIA

Have you ever heard the saying 'I'd die for a cup of tea'? In October 1747, 60 smugglers risked life and limb when they staged an armed robbery at a customs house, making off with a couple of tonnes of tea, leaving behind 39 casks of rum and brandy! Even though popular breakfast drinks back then were coffee, gin and beer, tea soon became the drink to start and end the day.

I'M WILLIAM, NOT HARRY!

In the 1750s handles were added to teacups to stop ladies from burning their fingers!

DRINKING TEA IS A PERK OF THE JOB.

Queen of thirst
Catherine of Braganza, who married King Charles II in 1662, was a tea diehard. When she landed in England from Portugal, she was gasping for a cup of tea. When none could be found, she was offered beer instead.

LARGER THAN LIFE

In the 1870s Tommy Lipton paraded a pig through his native Glasgow to promote the bacon in his first shop. When he became a tea tycoon in the 1890s, he upstaged himself. He paraded his tea on elephants!

THAT WAS A BIT OF A HIC-CUP!

The first cup of tea was sold in England in 1657.

GREAT BRITISH TEA

Storm in a teacup

Special teacups commemorate special events. A teacup of Prince William and Catherine Middleton was released just before their wedding in 2011, except the man on the cup was Prince Harry, his brother!

TEA MANNERS

Back in Victorian times, people poured their tea into the saucer to cool it down before sipping it. Today, the art of tea drinking is much more refined.

☆ Never stir your tea in circular motions with the teaspoon.
☆ Never clink the teaspoon against the cup.
☆ Place the teaspoon on the saucer behind the cup and to the right of the handle.
☆ Do not loop your fingers through the cup handle.
☆ Pour the milk in after the tea.
☆ Sip your tea – never slurp it!

Tea pickup

Afternoon tea came about thanks to the 7th Duchess of Bedford, who complained of a 'sinking feeling' during the late afternoon. Back then, people usually ate only breakfast and dinner. A pot of tea and a light snack helped revive and energise the Duchess.

WANT MORE?

BEST IN SHOW

Charles Cruft was the office boy in a company that sold dog biscuits but it was running the first Crufts Dog Show in 1891 that revealed his inner showman. Today, Crufts is the greatest dog show on Earth and fiercely competitive – it can be dog-eat-dog in the ring!

Top dog

With her flowing blonde locks, Elizabeth, a lhasa apso breed of dog, took Best in Show 2012, beating 21,000 other hopeful dogs. She also won Best of Breed and Best in Group. She took a well-deserved lap of honour before collecting her prizes.

SHOWS ON SHOW

No dogs are allowed at Crufts - unless they are invited!

Charles Cruft

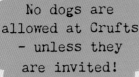

CAT SHOWS MAKE ME SO HAPPY.

Pampered pet
Now what kind of dog do you think Charles Cruft might have owned? Well, his wife often told the story that he didn't want to be seen to be favouring any particular breed of dog, so he had a cat instead.

I THINK 'CRUFTS' HAS A NICE RING TO IT!

No dogs allowed
In March 1894 Charles Cruft put on Crufts Cat Show. More than 600 cats entered, but the crowd attendance was low due to bad weather – it rained cats and dogs!

In 2012 an agility dog was disqualified for doing a doggy-do!

THE THINGS I DO TO KEEP THEM HAPPY...

Doggie names
Imagine how many Rovers, Bobs and Rosies could take part in Crufts. Luckily, the Kennel Club, which runs the show today, decided back in 1880 the way around it would be for a dog to have its own signature name. So Bob might become Sir Bones Baby-Face Bob.

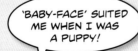

'BABY-FACE' SUITED ME WHEN I WAS A PUPPY!

Scruffy – not fluffy
If your dog looks more like the dog's dinner, then Scrufts Dog Show is the place for you. Started in 2000, the show is for crossbreed dogs. In other words, mongrels only.

WANT MORE?

Crufts official site ☆ www.crufts.org.uk

GREAT GAME OF GOLF

A rule of 1744: the tee must be on the ground!

I'M A HOTSHOT SCOT!

More than 250 years ago, the game of golf, as we know it today, swung into action in Scotland. Golf has come a long way since shepherds used to putt stones into rabbit holes with their crooks. This ancient game has seen its fair share of Scottish greats, from Mary, Queen of Scots to the father-and-son duo Old Tom and Young Tom Morris.

The hole story

The Royal and Ancient Golf Club of St Andrews dates back to 1754. Originally, the course had 22 holes. Then in 1764 it had 18 holes. Back then, some courses had as few as five holes!

WHAT IS HE WEARING?

Early golf shoes were hiking boots with tacks punched through the soles.

Old Tom and Young Tom

Old Tom Morris and Young Tom Morris became the oldest and youngest to play in the Open Championship. Old Tom was aged 74 years, 11 months and 24 days. Young Tom was aged 14 years, 4 months and 25 days!

FROM BAN TO FAN

Scotland's King James II banned golf in 1457. He thought it stopped soldiers from doing their archery practice. His grandson, James IV, practised his shots in secret and became the first royal golf nut!

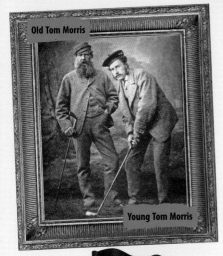

Old Tom Morris

Young Tom Morris

DUCK! FEATHER BALL COMING...

'Links' comes from an Old English word meaning 'rising ground'.

A deadly shot

Before 1848 golf balls were leather and stuffed with goose feathers. There was nothing soft about them. Legend has it that Old Tom Morris knew two people who had been killed by a flying feather-filled ball.

I'M A LADDIE, NOT A CADDIE!

Lady of the links

Mary, Queen of Scots was the first woman to regularly play golf. During her childhood in France, military cadets carried her golf clubs. The word 'caddie' came from 'cadet'.

WANT MORE?

IT'S ALL RIGHT, JEEVES,
THE EXPERIMENT WORKED.

Dr James Young Simpson

MEDICAL MARVELS

Have you heard the saying, 'No pain, no gain'?
Scottish doctor James Young Simpson probably felt
pain when he passed out and hit the floor in 1847.
He and his two assistants had taken a whiff and
a sniff of a liquid anaesthetic called chloroform.
But when Dr Simpson came round, he knew
the discovery was a real knock-out. Blood-curdling
cries from the operating tables might soon turn
to loud snoring instead!

Early surgeons
were barbers.
War surgeons
were nicknamed
'sawbones'.

MEDICAL MISHAPS

That's painful

Before anaesthetic came along, there were some interesting ways of getting a person ready for an operation. Some patients were hit over the head to make them unconscious. Another method was to pinch the nerves in the upper part of a leg or an arm and then apply cold water, ice or snow.

Pain of death

Chloroform was not always a medical marvel. The first anaesthetic-related death occurred in 1848. Poor 15-year-old English girl Hannah Greener died after having chloroform administered. She was only having a toenail removed!

IT WAS PAINLESS.

Queen Victoria

THIS WON'T HURT ONE LITTLE BIT.

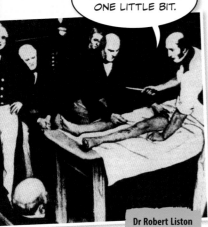

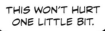
Dr Robert Liston

A painful shock

Before anaesthetic was invented, some patients died of shock during an operation. Some were given alcohol or opium to dull the pain, but many were just given something to bite on. Luckily, skilled surgeons could whip off a limb in about 30 seconds flat.

Posh pain

Queen Victoria gave anaesthetic the royal seal of approval when she had her eighth child in 1853. She was one of the first women to use chloroform during childbirth. Her physician was not keen on it because commoners used it!

A painful escape

Dr Robert Liston was a pioneering Scottish surgeon in Victorian times. During one operation, his patient ran off and locked himself in the toilet. Liston broke the door down and carried him back to the operating table!

PAIN BUT NO GAIN

In 1739, quack-doctor Joanna Stephens tricked people into parting with their money for her cure for painful bladder stones. The pills contained herbs, eggshells, soap and snail shells. Guess what? They didn't work.

WANT MORE?

History of Anaesthesia Society ✶ www.histansoc.org.uk

ODD BODS AND ODD BALLS

If 'eccentric' is your middle name, then how about these peculiar pastimes. You could snorkel in a bog (that's a wetland, not a toilet), chase after a runaway cheese or pull an ugly face without getting told off. These and other deviant diversions in Great Britain can make you laugh until you cry, or sometimes just make you cry.

GOOD GRIEF, WHERE'S MY TEETH?

HAVING A BALL!

The Royal Shrovetide Football Match is a peculiar pastime in the English town of Ashbourne. The match goes on for two days and hundreds of people join in. The teams have to chase the ball over fields, through streets and across water. That's because the goals are about 5km (3mi) apart.

What a sour face!

The sport of face-pulling, or gurning, started at the Egremont Crab Fair, which was first held in 1267. One story goes that when the Lord of Egremont gave away sour crab apples, people contorted their faces. Another story goes that the villagers would make a village idiot pull peculiar faces.

Cooper's Hill, Gloucestershire, England

A cheese roll

Break a leg! The crazy contestants need luck as they race down a steep grassy hill after a 3.5kg (7.7lb) wheel of Double Gloucester cheese. The cheese bounces and rolls at breakneck speed – and so do the contestants. People don't break their necks, but some sure break their arms and legs.

The first Shrovetide 'ball' may have been the severed head from an execution that was thrown into the crowd.

I'D RATHER BE GOALIE!

As hard as nails

The pastime of shin-kicking is still alive and kicking in England. Long ago, some shin-kickers used to toughen up their shins by banging them with coal hammers. People have been getting their kicks from this pastime for about 400 years.

Trouser trouble

One peculiar pastime has now been banned. Ferret leggers used to tie their trouser legs tightly at the ankles and then put two ferrets down their trousers. This pastime had some very peculiar rules. Ferret leggers could not be drunk and could not wear underwear!

IS THAT MAN LEGLESS?

Odd bods in odd bogs

The small town of Llanwrtyd Wells in Wales is proud of its peculiar pastime – bog snorkelling. Contestants can't use swimming strokes as they race through the bog. The contest does not always go swimmingly though. In 1995 the World Bog Snorkelling Competition was cancelled due to drought!

WANT MORE?

NESSIE

Scotland's most famous resident is not your typical celebrity. For one thing, she hates to be photographed. For another, she may, or may not, live in the murky waters of Loch Ness. And although she is often called Nessie, 'she' may not be a she at all! Nobody really knows much about the Loch Ness Monster. Even today, some people still believe there is an unsolved mystery lurking in the murk.

Diehard dinosaurs?
One popular belief is that Nessie is a plesiosaur. The theory goes that a family of these underwater uglies got locked in the loch when it formed 10,000 years ago. It's a good story – except that plesiosaurs died out 65 million years earlier!

ME? A MONSTER? WHAT A LAUGH!

DEEP AND DARK

Loch Ness contains more water than any other Scottish lake. In fact, it contains more water than all the lakes in England and Wales put together. Once upon a time, it was thought to harbour a kelpie. These mythical 'water horses' look like ordinary horses, except dripping wet and covered with water weeds!

Urquhart Castle, Loch Ness

'I brake for monsters'
The first modern sighting of Nessie was in 1933. A couple claimed to have seen a large creature with a long neck crossing the road in front of their car. It seems that road safety isn't one of Nessie's strong points!

What's in a name?
Naturalist Sir Peter Scott gave Nessie the scientific name *Nessiteras rhombopteryx*. It was pointed out that the letters could be rearranged to say 'monster hoax by Sir Peter S'.

OOPS!

CAN I BORROW A BROLLY?

Several unexplained sonar readings of large objects have been made in Loch Ness.

Famous fake
This 1934 photograph is an iconic image of Nessie. It is also a fake! Nessie was made using a lump of clay and a toy submarine.

MONSTER HUNTER
In 1969 monster hunter Dan Taylor went down in a submarine looking for Nessie. Unfortunately, he came up empty-handed. Even worse, the sub's hatch leaked so badly that Taylor had to use an umbrella to stay dry.

WANT MORE?

The legend of Nessie ☆ **www.nessie.co.uk**

BOND, JAMES BOND

Fictional British MI6 agent James Bond, code name 007, has been eliminating evil on the silver screen for more than 50 years. With spy gadgets like exploding toothpaste, shooting ski poles and cars with rocket launchers, Bond is more than a match for his enemies, especially if he's wearing his X-ray glasses designed for serious spying!

Double trouble
James Bond has a licence to kill, unlike real MI6 spies. Bond's creator, Ian Fleming, knew a real MI6 agent named Wilfred 'Biffy' Dunderdale. Biffy had a fondness for fast cars and pretty women. Sound familiar?

This Bond stunt set a record for the world's longest boat jump.

RECKON HE'S GOT A PILOT'S LICENCE?

NO, HE'S GOT A LICENCE TO KILL.

Hats off!
Bond movie baddies arm themselves with gadgets, too. Oddjob, the villain's bodyguard in *Goldfinger,* had a specially modified bowler hat with a razor in the rim. When thrown like a frisbee, it could slice and dice through flesh and bone.

Daniel Craig in Casino Royale

I NEED A REAR-VIEW MIRROR.

Sean Connery in the gyrocopter

The gadget man

In the Bond movies, the gadget maker is named Q. Wing Commander Kenneth Wallis is a real-life Q. He built this gyrocopter and was also a stuntman and double for Scottish actor Sean Connery in the 1967 Bond movie *You Only Live Twice*. During 81 flights Wallis dodged bullets in the air, while James Bond did his spy flying in the studio. A fan ruffled his shirt for special effects!

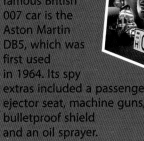

No ordinary car

Perhaps the most famous British 007 car is the Aston Martin DB5, which was first used in 1964. Its spy extras included a passenger ejector seat, machine guns, a bulletproof shield and an oil sprayer.

OT 03-65

KAPOW

007 TO HEAVEN

In the Bond movies, many apparently ordinary objects are packed with a powerful punch and are designed to kill:

☆ a briefcase with a sniper rifle, tear gas and a throwing knife (*From Russia With Love*)

☆ a watch that deflects speeding bullets (*Live and Let Die*)

☆ killer bagpipes with a machine gun (*The World Is Not Enough*)

☆ an explosive pen – click the top three times and four seconds later – BOOM! (*GoldenEye*)

WANT MORE?

Official James Bond site ☆ www.007.com

VOYAGE OF DISCOVERY

THIS IS WHERE I STARTED TO FEEL SEASICK.

The English scientist Charles Darwin caused a real fuss back in 1858. That's because he came up with a theory that modern species had evolved from earlier ones, which is not what most people believed. Darwin didn't just suddenly come up with his theory. He left Great Britain to go on a scientific expedition aboard HMS *Beagle*. The voyage lasted 4 years and 278 days, which gave him plenty of time to collect his thoughts, as well as boatloads of plants and animals!

In 1833 the *Beagle* even collected several prisoners!

COLLECTING CRAZE

Darwin's love of collecting soon caught on with some of the crew, but not everyone appreciated his butterfly and fishing nets all over the decks. The first lieutenant called Darwin a crazy flycatcher!

I THINK THESE BLUE FEET ARE A BOO-BOO.

Blue-footed booby

Bookworm Darwin
On the ship, Darwin spent hours reading in his hammock. That's because he was seasick for much of the trip.

At the Galápagos Islands, 30 giant tortoises were loaded onto the ship for eating.

Fur seal

Galápagos penguin

IS THAT SHARK OUR DINNER, OR ONE FOR DARWIN'S COLLECTION?

A naughty naturalist
Darwin was fascinated with the Galápagos Islands. He went for rides on the giant tortoises and remarked that the birds were so tame that he was able to push a hawk off a branch with his gun!

COLLECT AND KILL

When you collect animal specimens, you usually have to kill them. Darwin could make a live specimen a very dead one with a swift hit of his geological hammer, as some poor terns found out one day.

WANT MORE?

Dressing for danger
In 1939, Great Britain dished out millions of gas masks. Children between two and five got snazzy 'Mickey Mouse' ones that had blue rims around the eyes and a red flap for a nose. The masks were meant to make the children feel as if they were playing dress up.

IS MUM TAKING THE MICKEY?

CHILDREN OF THE WAR

War is a bore, especially for children. Imagine wearing a gas mask on a scorching day or being sent away from home with your teacher. That's what many children in Great Britain who lived through World War II had to do. They were made to live by catch phrases, such as 'it's patriotic to be shabby'. Just as well really, because many of them had to wear clothes made from old curtains!

Some horses even wore gas masks.

WHAT'S WELSH FOR YEE-HAA?

Evacuee heading to Wales

Whiteout in the blackout
To avoid being run over on the dark streets during the blackout, some children put white handkerchiefs into their pockets.

Children were urged to eat their carrots so they could see in the dark during the blackout.

MY WING WAS A BATHTUB.

For safe keeping
Many children were evacuated to the countryside for safety, but some were put on the wrong trains. In Anglesey, Wales, they expected 625 children, but 2468 jumped off the train instead!

On guard
Protecting the people of Great Britain was often done by the Home Guard, which was made up of young boys and old men. Their weapons included pitchforks, cricket bats and knives tied to broom handles.

Metal meltdown
Children went on house-to-house collections to gather up metal items, such as frying pans, kettles and tin baths. The metal items were melted down to make Spitfire planes.

Let's pig out
Food was usually scarce in the war, so people were encouraged to eat every bit of a pig, except its squeal!

WANT MORE?

World War II ☆ www.bbc.co.uk/schools/primaryhistory/world_war2

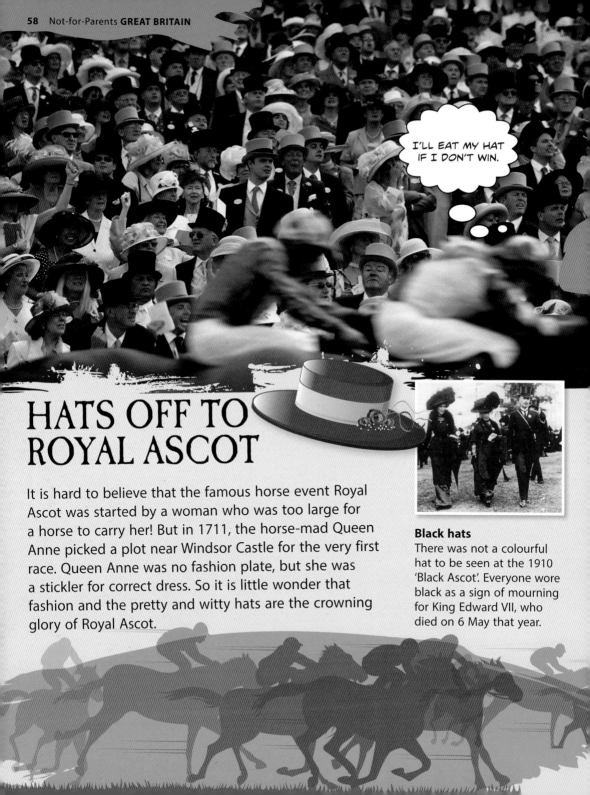

I'LL EAT MY HAT IF I DON'T WIN.

HATS OFF TO ROYAL ASCOT

It is hard to believe that the famous horse event Royal Ascot was started by a woman who was too large for a horse to carry her! But in 1711, the horse-mad Queen Anne picked a plot near Windsor Castle for the very first race. Queen Anne was no fashion plate, but she was a stickler for correct dress. So it is little wonder that fashion and the pretty and witty hats are the crowning glory of Royal Ascot.

Black hats
There was not a colourful hat to be seen at the 1910 'Black Ascot'. Everyone wore black as a sign of mourning for King Edward VII, who died on 6 May that year.

I'LL BET SHE'LL WEAR BLUE TOMORROW.

A hat hunch
Betting is big business at Royal Ascot. Some punters place bets on which colour hat Queen Elizabeth will wear.

At Ascot, children under 16 don't have to wear hats.

TAKE THAT, HAT!
Top hats don't spook the horses at Ascot, but in 1797 John Hetherington almost caused a stampede in the street when he wore one for the first time. Children screamed and dogs yelped in fright.

The mad hatter
Mrs Gertrude Shilling was nicknamed the 'Ascot Mascot'. Her hats were outrageous – and BIG! Punters made bets on whether her hats would fit between the Royal Enclosure gates.

Fancy hats (but not fancy dress) are permitted at Ascot.

Hair hat, now and then
In 2011 this hat caused as much fuss at Royal Ascot as the Duchess of Devonshire's creations did in the late 1700s. The Duchess made a 1m (3ft) tall hair tower using her own hair and horsehair!

WANT MORE?

Royal Ascot official site ☆ www.ascot.co.uk

RUGBY RULES!

Some say that the game of rugby as we know it today started at Rugby School in England. The story goes that a 16-year-old boy named William Webb Ellis, who sometimes showed little regard for rules on the sporting field, picked up the ball and ran with it. The year was 1823, and doing that was just not the done thing. However, the run soon turned to a rule, and players have been following the rule ever since.

Statue of William Webb Ellis at Rugby School

I'M DOING A WILLIAM WEBB ELLIS AND RUNNING WITH THE BALL.

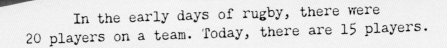

In the early days of rugby, there were 20 players on a team. Today, there are 15 players.

On the ball
Early rugby balls were round. It is believed that the oval shape came about because of the pigs' bladders that were used to make the ball. The inflated bladders were covered with four leather panels. Today, balls must still be oval with four panels.

THEY MADE A PIG'S EAR OF THAT TACKLE.

Clothing code
Cardiff Rugby Football Club was founded in 1876. Its first uniform was a black shirt with a skull and crossbones emblem on it. That's until some parents complained it was unsuitable for children.

Twickenham Stadium

Play on
One of the most famous rugby grounds is Twickenham Stadium in England. It is sometimes called the 'cabbage patch' because it was built on a site that was partly a market garden. Today, players are officially allowed to play on grass, sand, clay, fake grass and even snow.

PUNCHING'S ILLEGAL. TRY SHIN-KICKING.

GET YOUR KICKS

Rugby players can run with the ball, pass it or kick it. Long ago a different kind of kicking took place. It was called 'hacking', which was the deliberate kicking of an opponent's shins. It was banned in 1871, but Rugby School allowed it for 10 more years. Some clubs allowed just five minutes of hacking at the end of the game.

WANT MORE?

Rules of the game of Rugby Union ☆ www.irblaws.com

OFF THE PAGE

JK Rowling was on a slow train to London when a bespectacled boy wizard popped into her head. Stuck on the train, Rowling learnt an important lesson for any writer: never go anywhere without a pen! She eventually made it home, and Harry Potter made it onto the page and the big screen. But the magic of Harry Potter goes way beyond books and movies.

> I USUALLY GET MY HOUSE-ELF TO SIGN THEM.

JK Rowling has been made into a special one-off Barbie doll.

POTTERING ABOUT

It took JK Rowling five years to finish the first Harry Potter book, writing in cafes and in the evenings. She typed it up on an old-fashioned typewriter, then had to retype it all double-spaced! The finished book was rejected eight times before finally being published in 1997.

> DEWEY DECIMAL? I THOUGHT YOU SAID 'DECIBEL'!

Rock 'n' Rowling
When two brothers started playing songs based on Harry Potter, they invented a new musical genre called 'wizard rock'. Apart from their songs and Hogwarts-themed outfits, Harry and the Potters are notable for playing mainly in libraries. Quiet, please!

Hi-tech Harry
Fancy some virtual Voldemort or digital Dumbledore? In 2012 Harry Potter went online with a bewitching new website, www.pottermore.com.

Harijs Poters?
What do people in Latvia, Azerbaijan and at least 65 other countries have in common? They can all read Harry Potter translated into their native language.

Scarf ace
Bradford City football club had some money troubles, but a sprinkle of Harry Potter magic helped out. Sales of the club scarf rocketed after Potter fans discovered it was in Gryffindor house colours!

SPELLING MISTAKE!
Magic charms like *Wingardium Leviosa* didn't just make feathers accidentally explode – they caused a boom in Latin learning, too. The number of British schools offering Latin classes has more than tripled since the Harry Potter books first came out.

Brooms up
At the annual Quidditch World Cup, real-life teams dodge bludgers and try to get the quaffle through the hoop while holding a broomstick between their legs. It may not be actual magic, but these muggles aren't mucking about!

WANT MORE?

WHAT'S THE BIG IDEA?

Imagine setting out to build the largest ships and bridges in the world. Everything about Isambard Kingdom Brunel was larger than life, including his outlandish name. Even his mistakes were monumental. Brunel was the greatest engineer in an age when bigger usually meant better. And the biggest ideas of all came from the amazing brain beneath Brunel's famous top hat.

YOU'RE SURE THESE CHAINS DON'T MAKE ME LOOK SMALL?

IT WASN'T ME, I ASSURE YOU!

Whiffy work
Brunel's first big job was helping his father build a tunnel beneath the River Thames. It was dangerous work – as well as sudden floods, the fumes from leaking sewage were so strong they would knock the workers unconscious!

Off the tracks
Brunel was Chief Engineer on the Great Western Railway from London to Bristol. He made the trains wider than usual for extra luxury and speed. But the wide trains wouldn't fit on ordinary tracks, so the entire line had to be ripped up and replaced.

A 2002 poll named Brunel the second-greatest Briton of all time.

MEGA-FLOPS

Brunel's successes were celebrated, but his disasters were just as legendary.

The ship that stuck
When it was built, Brunel's *Great Eastern* was the largest ship ever made. Its launch was watched by a crowd of three million. But the heavy iron ship immediately sank into the mud and took three months to refloat.

The train that sucked
Brunel's 'atmospheric railway' used suction instead of engines to pull the trains. Sadly, it really did suck – especially when the suction pipe was eaten by rats!

Design skulduggery
In 1830 Brunel won a contest to design the Clifton Suspension Bridge in Bristol. But his bridge almost didn't get made. The judge initially rejected Brunel's design and declared himself the winner!

WANT MORE?

Brunel's story ☆ www.brunel.ac.uk/about/history/isambard-kingdom-brunel

BEATLE MANIA

In 1963 four musicians from Liverpool released a song called 'She Loves You'. It went to the top of the British charts and stayed there, breaking all previous records. Soon almost everyone in the world had heard of The Beatles. The band split up just six years later, but in that time they recorded some of the most famous songs of the century and changed the face of popular music. 'Yeah, yeah, yeah!'

What's that sound?
Before The Beatles, no one had ever seen such fanatical fans. People who wanted to hear them play in concert were disappointed – they couldn't hear the music above all the screaming.

THIS GUITAR'S GOING TO MAKE ME A STAR!

The 'Fab Four'
The Beatles were Paul McCartney, Ringo Starr, George Harrison and John Lennon. They all sang and they all played guitar except Ringo, who was the drummer. This photo shows them when they first became famous. Later they dropped the black suits and started wearing much more colourful hippy-style clothes.

AM I DREAMING OR JUST SCREAMING?

Souvenir sign
The Beatles named their 11th album *Abbey Road* – which is an actual road in London. After the album was released the street sign kept disappearing. Eventually the local council put it high up on a building – out of the reach of thieving fans.

ABBEY ROAD NW8
CITY OF WESTMINSTER

Before settling on 'The Beatles', the band was named 'The Blackjacks', 'The Quarrymen' and 'Johnny and the Moondogs'.

BREAKING RECORDS

Pricey piano
In 2000 singer George Michael bought John Lennon's piano, the one he used to write the song 'Imagine'. Michael paid £1.45 million ($2.1 million). Imagine!

Top tunes
The Beatles' music finally made it onto iTunes in November 2010. In the first week alone, 2 million songs and 450,000 albums were sold.

Extreme makeover
John Lennon had a Rolls-Royce that was originally black but got a 'psychedelic' paint job. It was auctioned in 1985. The auction house estimated its value as $300,000. It sold for $2.29 million!

WANT MORE?

Which Beatle are you? ✭ www.liverpoolmuseums.org.uk/online/games/beatles

ROBIN WHO?

Robin Hood was the forest-dwelling outlaw who stole from the rich and gave to the poor. But was he just a character in some old stories, or did he actually live? Was he a medieval nobleman or just a petty thief? Did he really give everything away, or keep it for himself and his band of Merry Men? The answers may surprise you.

Robin of Barnsdale
'Robin Hood in Sherwood stood' goes an old saying. But some people think Robin Hood's leafy lair was not Sherwood Forest but Barnsdale Wood, 80km (50mi) up the road in Yorkshire. One Yorkshire MP demanded that Nottingham take down all signs calling itself 'Robin Hood Country'!

NOTTINGHAMSHIRE

BRITISH RAILWAYS   SEE ENGLAND BY RAIL

Robin Hoodlum
The earliest Robin Hood stories are in a collection called 'A Gest of Robyn Hode'. The Robin Hood in these tales is a ruthless robber who doesn't think twice about chopping off the Sheriff of Nottingham's head!

Acorny tale
According to local legend, the Major Oak in Sherwood Forest was Robin Hood's shelter. If true, then Robin Hood must have been very small – the famous old oak would have been just an acorn in Robin's time!

Monk mayhem
As the Robin Hood legend grew, so did his band of Merry Men. One of the merriest was Friar Tuck – but the jolly monk had a dark secret. He was based on a real-life chaplain who called himself Frere Tuk and went on a murderous crime spree!

ROGUES' GALLERY
Will the real Robin Hood please stand up? Here are a few of the main suspects.

The Nobleman
When Fulk Fitzwarin's castle was confiscated by King John, he moved to a nearby forest and became a robber alongside a friend named John.

IT'S NOT MY FULK...

THE NAME'S ROBIN HOOD, NOT LITTLE RED RIDING HOOD!

The Brigand
Roger Godberd led a band of thieves in Sherwood Forest. Like Robin Hood, he was caught by the Sheriff of Nottingham. Unlike Robin, he kept his ill-gotten gains for himself.

The Monk
Eustace the Monk lived in a French forest and loved making life difficult for the local lord. A later career as a pirate was cut short – by an enemy axe!

I'M A CHEEKY MONKIE!

THIS SWORD IS PERFECT FOR CLEANING FINGERNAILS.

The Fugitive
In 1225 a man named 'Robert Hod' was on the run from the law in Yorkshire. The hunt for the infamous outlaw was led by a future Sheriff of Nottingham.

WANT MORE?

QUEENS OF THE COURT

Tennis was the game of kings. Henry VIII was so fond of the game that he even played it while one of his wives was executed. But before long, queens of the court (the tennis court, that is) soon smashed into history. Women first hit the courts at Wimbledon in 1884. There were 13 of them, and they battled it out for the grand prize of a silver flower basket!

ADVANTAGE... ME!

Miss Lottie Dod

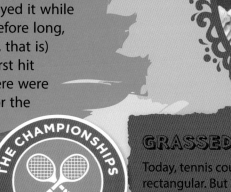

OVER NOT OUT!

THE CHAMPIONSHIPS WIMBLEDON

GRASSED UP

Today, tennis courts are rectangular. But in 1874, Major Walter Clopton Wingfield, the father of modern tennis, featured an hourglass-shaped court in his famous rule book.

Court care
Maintaining the grass courts at Wimbledon is serious stuff. The grass has to be just 8mm (0.3in) tall, and in winter, electric fences stop foxes from stepping on the grass on some courts!

Tennis star
Give a hand to English player Muriel Robb. She was the first woman to serve overhand. She also won her singles match at Wimbledon in 1902 after playing 53 games over two days!

In 1874 tennis was called Sphairistike, or 'Sticky' for short.

THAT GROUNDSMAN HAS OUTFOXED ME.

Hemmed in

Long ago, people were outraged when women wore tennis skirts above the ankles. Miss Lottie Dod was lucky though. When she won Wimbledon in 1887, she was a youngster. Back then, children were allowed to wear shorter skirts.

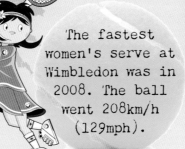

The fastest women's serve at Wimbledon was in 2008. The ball went 208km/h (129mph).

COURT TALK

★ 1884 First women's singles champion: Maud Watson, defeating her older sister

★ 1887 Youngest women's singles champion: Miss Lottie Dod; 15 years and 285 days

★ 1908 Oldest women's singles champion: Mrs Charlotte Sterry; 37 years and 282 days

★ 1922 Oldest women's singles competitor: Mrs AE O'Neill; 54 years and 304 days

★ 1977 Last British woman to win: Virginia Wade

Start the ball rolling

At Wimbledon, 1977 was a good year. That's when ball girls made their first appearance, but they had to wait till 1985 before they could strut their stuff on Centre Court.

Killer on the court

In the late 1870s, women played tennis in long petticoats and tight corsets. Often the restrictive corsets were stained with blood by the end of the game!

WANT MORE?

Wimbledon official site ★ www.wimbledon.com

A DARING DESIGNER

Vivienne Westwood was a bit of a wild child. On her first day at nursery school, when she saw a long queue outside the girls' toilet, Vivienne marched off to the boys' toilet instead. Back then it might have got her a slap from her teacher, but when the daring girl grew up and started creating scandalous outfits for her shop, she slapped the face of the establishment right back. The bold fashion designer became the Queen of Outrageous, creating street fashion for Great Britain and high fashion for the catwalk.

FASHION IS NOT A CRIME!

Gloomy days
Sometimes life was pretty hard for Vivienne. When she reopened her Worlds End shop in July 1986, the gas and electricity were not connected. People had to shop for clothes by torch and candlelight.

Vivienne Westwood, 1977

Vivienne was even arrested for some of her outrageous designs.

Catwalks and dogs

In the early days of her catwalk shows, Vivienne sometimes ran two hours late. Once a show was delayed because the seamstress bringing the clothes had spent the morning chasing her escaped dog around the neighbourhood!

WHEN I GROW UP I WANT TO WORK FOR VIVIENNE.

Vivienne grew up with the wartime motto of 'make do and mend'.

The kitchen cardigan

One unusual design was something Vivienne called the 'kitchen sink' cardigan. Probably a good name, because it was made from a dishcloth. The buttons were made from the metal lids of kitchen-scourer powder tins.

I WISH I DIDN'T END UP ON A T-SHIRT.

2012 Vivienne Westwood show

Chicken lickin' designs

In the 1970s Vivienne decorated T-shirts with chicken bones. She tied the bones onto the cloth with chains and spelt out words such as 'Rock'.

WANT MORE?

Vivienne Westwood official site ☆ www.viviennewestwood.co.uk

A REGAL RULER

Princess Elizabeth caused a real stir when she was born in 1533. Her father, King Henry VIII, was so pipped that she was a girl that he didn't even go to her christening. He had wanted a son, to be king after him. Little did he know that after Elizabeth became Queen of England in 1558, she ruled with the heart and stomach of a king.

JUST CALL ME BUSY LIZZY!

Hot temper
Elizabeth I never married. She was 'married' to England instead. It might have been just as well. She usually liked to get her own way. When she got angry, she would box people's ears or throw her shoes at them.

DRESSED FOR SUCCESS
Early in her reign, Elizabeth realised that an appearance of success was important. She wore exquisite clothes and jewellery so that she looked the part of queen. In other words, she was a 'power dresser'.

Royal road trips

Elizabeth went on about 25 regional tours around England during her reign to keep in touch with her subjects. She often went on horseback. Elizabeth had a horse that matched her hair. Its tail and mane were dyed orange!

A loyal loo

Sir John Harington, Elizabeth's godson, invented a very special 'throne' for the queen. It was a flush toilet. Talk about a royal flush!

NO ONE IS GOING TO HAVE MY THRONE.

THE KINGPIN QUEEN

Elizabeth I was a wise queen. Her reign is sometimes referred to as the 'Golden Age' because during her rule she turned England into a great nation.

✯ encouraged trade expansion; established the East India Company in 1600

✯ defeated the Spanish when they invaded England in 1588

✯ promoted the arts; attended the first performance of William Shakespeare's *A Midsummer Night's Dream*

A robbing ruler?

Elizabeth did not like to spend money, but she loved receiving luxurious gifts. When she toured England, her hosts showered her with presents. If Elizabeth didn't like them, she just took what she liked from her host's house.

Elizabeth ruled for 45 years.

Sweet gifts

Courtiers gave their beloved queen gifts of sweets. Elizabeth ate so many sweets that her teeth turned black. To be just like her, the Queen's ladies even blackened their teeth.

WANT MORE?

Guinness World Records came about because of an argument. Sir Hugh Beaver was bird shooting in 1951 when the topic of which game bird in Europe was the fastest came up. Later, while hunting through encyclopedias, the answer wasn't found. But Sir Hugh, the boss of Guinness Brewery, realised that a book of records could be just the thing to settle pub arguments. Along came the fact-finding English editors and twins Ross and Norris McWhirter, who turned the book into the source for facts, figures and far-out, freaky feats.

OLDEST, SMALLEST, LOUDEST

LARGEST

997, 998, 999...

THERE'S PLENTY OF LEG ROOM.

TALLEST

SMALLEST

Gnome home
Ann Atkin of Devon has plenty to keep her company. That's because she has the world's largest collection of gnomes and pixies. Back in March 2011, she had a staggering 2042 of them.

Tallest
In 2011 Englishman Paul 'Tiny' Sturgess was the world's tallest professional basketball player.

Smallest
In 2009 English inventor Perry Watkins got the record for the world's smallest roadworthy car.

The trivia twins

The McWhirter twins were the perfect pair to compile the *Guinness World Records*. They had almost photographic memories, and even as children they collected facts and figures.

TALLEST...

Guinness World Records itself holds a world record. It is the best-selling copyrighted book series of all time!

BEST-SELLING

OLDEST

Oldest and boldest

Scottish great grandmother and daredevil Peggy McAlpine was 104 years old when she became the world's oldest paraglider in 2012.

One record that keeps getting beaten is the oldest person in the world.

BEAT THAT!

* **Oldest vomit:**
  the fossilised vomit of an ichthyosaur was found in Peterborough in 2002

* **Shortest street:**
  Ebenezer Place, Wick, Caithness, Scotland, is 2.05m (6.7ft) long

* **Oldest football:**
  more than 435 years old; found in the mid-1970s in a bedroom that Mary, Queen of Scots used

* **Fastest pantomime:**
  lasted 5 minutes and 50 seconds; performed in London on 16 April 2009

* **Oldest British queen:**
  Queen Elizabeth II, who beat Queen Victoria on 21 December 2007

* **Loudest purr:**
  Smokey the cat from Northampton in 2010 recorded 67.7dB (that's louder than a dishwasher)!

WANT MORE?

Palace of Holyrood House

The ghost of 'Bald Agnes' Sampson – accused of being a witch – is said to haunt the palace.

YOU WOULD NOT BELIEVE THE THINGS I'VE SEEN.

No Hollywood ending

Mary, Queen of Scots married two of her three husbands at the Palace of Holyrood House in Edinburgh. In 1566 her private secretary was murdered there, in front of Mary. He'd been having supper with her. Sounds safe enough!

ROYAL RETREATS

There is definitely no chance of roughing it in the royal palaces of Great Britain today. Many of them were once drafty old castles, but with a bit of a spruce up and exquisite drapes and furniture, they became homely havens for the royals to loll about in luxury. However, some of the residences during their long history have not always been a piece of paradise.

WHAT'S THAT HORRID SMELL?

A right royal smell

In 1327 Edward II was imprisoned in Berkeley Castle in England. He didn't have the best room. Rotting cattle carcasses were thrown into a deep hole near his cell. Edward's captors were hoping he would be poisoned by the toxic stench. He wasn't.

An elephant is buried in the grounds of the Tower of London.

Polar prisoner

For 600 years the Tower of London housed the Royal Menagerie, including three leopards, an elephant and a polar bear. The bear was allowed to fish on the River Thames, but it was always on an iron chain!

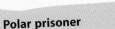

I HAVEN'T SEEN A BOY ESCAPE, BUT A GIRL SHOT PAST.

Great escape

As a child, King James II was held prisoner at St James's Palace in London, although thanks to a game of hide-and-seek with his siblings, he managed to escape in 1648. He dressed up as a girl!

WANT MORE?

Royal residences ☆ www.royal.gov.uk/theroyalresidences/reschannel.aspx

LOUD AND PROUD

In Wales, they like to do things differently. They have an alphabet with 28 letters, names that nobody else can pronounce and a festival where the top prize is a chair! The Welsh are proud of their language and culture, and the Eisteddfod (*eye-steth-vod*) is where they celebrate it. So, welcome to the Eisteddfod, or as they say in Wales, Croeso i'r Eisteddfod (*kroy-so ear eye-steth-vod*)!

I'M SURE I'VE FORGOTTEN SOMETHING...

The Welsh word for Wales is Cymru (kum-ree).

Show time

The National Eisteddfod is held each August at a different place in Wales. Welsh poets, musicians and artists come to strut their stuff and compete for prizes. The kids' version, called the Urdd (*urth*) Eisteddfod, is the biggest youth festival in Europe.

Who's allowed?

Wales is famous for its male-voice choirs, but Only Boys Aloud is special – it is made up of boys aged 14 to 19 who practise at rugby clubs across Wales. Their first-ever performance was on the opening night of the 2010 National Eisteddfod. A new choir called Only Kids Aloud started in 2012!

Only Kids Aloud

Champion's chair

At each Eisteddfod, a specially made chair is awarded to the writer of the best 'awdl' – a kind of Welsh poem. So if someone at an Eisteddfod asks you to take a seat, you may have won the top prize!

HMM, WHAT RHYMES WITH EISTEDDFOD?

The black chair

Hedd Wyn won the poetry prize at the 1917 National Eisteddfod, but he never got to sit in the winner's chair. He had been killed six weeks earlier in the trenches of World War I. His chair was draped in a black shroud, and ever since, that year's festival has been called the Eisteddfod of the Black Chair.

GONE TO PATAGONIA

At the Patagonian Eisteddfod in South America, everyone speaks Welsh with a Spanish accent! A Welsh colony was founded in southern Argentina in 1865, and people have spoken Welsh there ever since.

WANT MORE?

The National Eisteddfod of Wales ☆ www.eisteddfod.org.uk/english

THE HOME OF GADGETS

Scottish engineer John Logie Baird whipped up the first
television with a tea chest, a hatbox lid, a knitting needle
and other bits and bobs found in junk shops and junk yards.
But if it hadn't been for the vision of gadget gurus such as
Baird, our homes would be much emptier places.

On the ball
This Dyson vacuum
cleaner rolls on a ball
rather than four wheels.
Dyson also invented
a wheelbarrow with
no wheel and a fan
with no blades!

Dream machine
English inventor James Dyson is famous for
inventing vacuum cleaners. His first design took
five years and 5127 prototypes to perfect.

INVENTION TIME

Many household items were invented
by people from Great Britain.

1830
Reel lawnmower
Edwin Budding,
English inventor

1876
Telephone
Alexander Graham Bell,
Scottish inventor

1901
Electric vacuum cleaner
Hubert Cecil Booth,
English inventor

1963
Lava lamp
Edward Craven Walker,
English inventor

Television demo

John Logie Baird demonstrated his television for the first time in a London department store in 1925. He named his contraption the 'Televisor'.

> Baird tried to invent a razor that never went blunt, but cut himself so badly that he gave up.

> I COULD DO WITH ANOTHER KNITTING NEEDLE.

CAT AND MOUSE GADGETS

> THAT CAT-FLAP IS A TRAP!

Cat contraption

Arthur Paul Pedrick was an eccentric English inventor. He filed more than 160 patent applications, but his cat-flap that let only ginger cats in might have been one of the stranger ones. It was designed to keep Blackie, the next-door cat, out!

> I'LL HAVE THAT CHEESE IN A SNAP.

www-Wicked!

Two Englishmen were early techno whizzes. Charles Babbage invented the first mechanical computer, and Tim Berners-Lee devised the World Wide Web. Wow!

Mouse in the house?

Englishman James Henry Atkinson invented a mousetrap called the 'Little Nipper'. It still holds the record for the fastest snapping action. Atkinson sold the rights to his invention to the Welsh company Procter Brothers, which sold the traps from 1897.

WANT MORE?

John Logie Baird ★ www.bairdtelevision.com

TOTALLY GREAT

Ever since people have lived on the island of Great Britain, they have tried to divide it up. Massive walls were built, proud nations rose up and wars were fought. Today, England, Scotland and Wales form Great Britain, while Great Britain and Northern Ireland belong to the United Kingdom. But they have not always been very united!

THERE ARE TOO MANY PICTS ROMAN AROUND!

1st–4th C   The Empire strikes
The Romans conquer Great Britain. Emperor Hadrian builds a massive stone wall to keep out the Picts in the north. The Picts go off and form Scotland with the Gaels.

1999   Back in business
The Scottish Parliament reopens after a 292-year break, and Wales gets its own parliament, the Welsh Assembly.

I'M A STONE...

...AND I'M A SCONE!

1950   Stone gone!
Four Scottish students sneak into Westminster Abbey and remove the famous Stone of Scone. The ceremonial stone was taken from Scotland in 1296. But the break-in turns into a break-up when the stone splits in two!

2011   Football fuss
When a combined Great Britain football team is announced for the 2012 Olympics, the only thing kicked off is a huge row. Scotland and Wales don't even turn up for the talks!

KEEP OFFA MY LAND!

Great Britain is the eighth largest island in the world.

1282 **Llywelyn loses his head**
Llywelyn the Last of Wales is killed by the English. His head is stuck on a spike at the Tower of London and stays there for 25 years.

8th C **Pests in the west**
After the Romans leave, Anglo-Saxons take over. King Offa gets so fed up with his western neighbours that he builds a 100km (60mi) wall to keep them at bay. The land to the west of Offa's Dyke becomes Wales.

1603 **Royal double**
Well, 25 July must be a confusing day for King James VI of Scotland, because that's the day he is also crowned James I of England! It is the first time both countries have shared the same monarch.

I'M 'ENRY THE EIGHTH, I AM!

1314 **A splitting headache**
Fighting the English at the Battle of Bannockburn, the Scots get off to a 'head start' when their king, Robert the Bruce, buries his axe in an English nobleman's skull!

1543 **Henry in a hurry**
Henry VIII declares war on Scotland to force the Scots to let his son marry the Scottish queen. At the time, Prince Edward is only six years old and Queen Mary is still a baby.

WANT MORE?

British history in games and quizzes ☆ www.bbc.co.uk/history/forkids

A SCHOOL OF TRADITION

If your school was almost 600 years old, then you would expect a tradition or two. Luckily, for the pupils at Eton College today, many of them no longer exist. Eton is one of the most famous private (called public) schools in England. It is frightfully posh, but that is a far cry from its more humble beginnings. King Henry VI founded the school in 1440, as he was keen to give 70 poor boys a free education. It might have been free, but at times it certainly wasn't fun!

The wall tradition
The Wall Game is a unique tradition that takes place on St Andrew's Day. It is a football game played on a long, narrow strip along the wall, which was built in 1717. Goals are rarely scored. In fact, the last goal was in 1909.

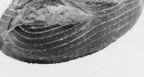

Unsupervised mayhem
In the early days, the 70 Scholars were locked, unsupervised, in their dormitory from 8:00 p.m. till the next morning. They often went on rat-hunts, as the rats were locked in, too!

An eatin' education
Boarders traditionally complain about school food, but spare a thought for the 70 poor boys, called Scholars, who lived at Eton in the early days. They didn't get fed at all on Fridays, as it was a day of fasting.

Bully tactics
Bullying was once a tradition. It wasn't great to be the new boys. They were tossed up in blankets. One poor lad was scalped when he accidentally landed on a bedpost!

Sport slackers

If you were a rower at Eton, you were called a Wet Bob.
If you were a cricketer, you were a Dry Bob. If you didn't
play cricket or do rowing, then you were a Slack Bob!

Long ago, during
the day the boys were
allowed to speak
only Latin.

ABSOLUTUM
DOMINIUM!

Flowery traditions

On 4 June Eton rowers wear boater
hats decorated with flowers and take
part in the Procession of Boats. Many
years ago, just for fun, boys rowed
up and down the river dressed in
fancy dress. The first recorded rowing
pageant took place on 4 June 1793.

Stone the crows

Some Eton traditions have been
banned. In the past, on Shrove
Tuesday, the cook would tie
a crow to a door along with
a pancake. The aim of the
game was to throw things
at the crow until it died!

I SAY,
ARE THEY ETON OR
HARROW BOYS?

Eton vs Harrow

A tradition that is still followed is that Eton takes part
in a cricket clash against its rival Harrow at Lord's
cricket ground. The Eton boys wore top hats and tails,
at least until they got changed into their cricket kit.

WANT
MORE?

Famous people who attended Eton ☆ www.etoncollege.com/ListsOfFamousOEs.aspx

PIER PLEASURE

Palace Pier in Brighton was designed to be the people's palace above the sea. Long ago, when swimming or floating in the ocean was considered to be an extremely unnatural activity, people instead flocked to Brighton's piers – the pleasure domes of the English seaside.

About 67,000 lights illuminate the Palace Pier at night.

Pier performances
In 1888 the Brighton West Pier Orchestra entertained people on the pier. But in 1889, people paid to watch Miss Louie Webb there as well. She sat in a glass tank containing water, where she would sew, write and eat sponge cake, all while underwater!

I FEEL LIKE PUNCHING SOMEONE.

Packed with a punch

Punch and Judy puppet shows came to England in 1662. Today, this puppet show might not be exactly suitable for children. Punch beats his child and argues with his wife. Sometimes he even kills her.

Sea train

This looks like a pier, but it is a train track on stilts. The electric train ride was built in Brighton in 1896 and was nicknamed the Daddy-long-legs. It was probably not that entertaining when a wave came.

DON'T YOU LOVE THE SPECIAL EFFECTS?

Entertainers galore

Even though the general public didn't go swimming or diving, it didn't stop the entertainers. In 1868 there was a one-legged swimmer who ate breakfast on the water. In the early 1900s some performers were famous for their bicycle-dive acts in which they rode their bikes off the pier.

WANT MORE?

RISE UP!

It is 1296, and Scotland is in peril. The English king, Edward I, has decided Scotland is his for the taking – but an unknown Scotsman has other ideas. William Wallace hastily assembles a band of rebels and fights back with cunning and bravery. Sadly, Wallace will eventually meet a sticky end, but the legend of the Scottish freedom fighter lives on.

I THINK MY PANTS ARE ON FIRE!

GIBSON

BRAVEHEART

Movie muddle
The movie *Braveheart* supposedly tells the story of William Wallace, but often gets its facts wrong – starting with the title! The name 'Braveheart' was not given to Wallace, but to another Scottish warrior, Robert the Bruce.

Stirling Bridge

Swept away
A year after the English invasion, Wallace and his ragtag army faced the English across the River Forth at Stirling. They were outnumbered ten to one, but Wallace had a plan. As the enemy began crossing Stirling Bridge, he attacked. In the havoc, the narrow bridge collapsed, taking the English soldiers with it.

YOU CAN'T GET GOOD SERVANTS THESE DAYS.

Wallace being led to trial

OFF WITH HIS HEAD

Rebels could expect a nasty end if caught. William Wallace was hanged, drawn and quartered. A famous English rebel, Oliver Cromwell, died before he could be executed. But after his death, his body was dug up and his head chopped off and stuck on a pole. It was stolen by a passerby, who took it home and hid it in a chimney!

Sneaky servant
Wallace became a feared guerilla fighter, but was badly beaten at the Battle of Falkirk. Even after Scotland and England had declared a truce, he refused to surrender. He fought on for years until he was betrayed by a servant and taken to London to be put on trial.

Mel Gibson in the movie Braveheart

a. He was the son of a nobleman. True or false?

b. He was 2.1m (7ft) tall and once fought a lion in France! True or false?

c. He killed three soldiers in an argument over a fish. True or false?

d. He was a skilled archer. True or false?

i. His legend was written down by a minstrel named Blind Harry. True or false?

h. He killed the Sheriff of Lanark to avenge the murder of his wife. True or false?

e. He spoke English, French, Gaelic and Latin. True or false?

g. He wore a kilt. True or false?

f. He wore a belt made from the skin of one of his enemies. True or false?

The man and the myth
The full facts of William Wallace's life may never be known, but all kinds of fantastic stories swirl around him. Sort the myth from the reality.

Answers
a. True. **b.** False, although he was very tall. **c.** True – his seal depicts an archer's bow. **e.** True. **f.** Probably just a myth! **g.** False – kilts weren't invented yet. **h.** False – Wallace killed the Sheriff, but there is no proof he was ever married. **i.** True, but some experts believe Harry was neither blind, nor called Harry!

WANT MORE?
The story of Robert the Bruce, the real 'Braveheart' ☆ www.brucetrust.co.uk

ROYALS ON THE ROAD

On her many travels, the Queen has got from A to B in anything from a barge to an elephant. But back home in Great Britain, she usually hits the road in one of her cars or carriages. Her garage, the Royal Mews at Buckingham Palace, houses numerous cars, carriages and coaches, but these regal runabouts are certainly not your run-of-the-mill wheel mobiles!

A golden oldie

The oldest coach in the Royal Collection is the Golden State Coach, which is a hand-me-down from King George III. He wanted it for his coronation, but it wasn't ready in time. It first rolled onto the road in 1762.

I HOPE IT DOESN'T TURN INTO A PUMPKIN.

Limos in livery

The Queen has eight state limousines to use for official occasions: two Bentleys, three Rolls-Royces and three Daimlers. The oldest car is a 1950 Rolls-Royce Phantom IV. They are all painted claret.

There are more than 100 carriages and coaches in the Royal Collection.

Number one
The Queen could afford personalised number plates, but she doesn't have to bother. The state cars don't need number plates at all.

WAIT UP, DEAR.

A regal roller
The Queen's cars often have special features, such as a high roof (allowing her to wear tall hats) and rear doors that open backwards. They help her to get in and out of the car in a dignified fashion!

By law, the Queen does not need a driver's licence.

Wheely slow
Even the Queen has to follow the speed limits on the road. When she drives in a procession, her car goes at a snail's pace. It often drives as slowly as 5 km/h (3 mph).

Added extras
The Queen had a Daimler car that had dog-friendly fittings. The magazine holders next to the seats had covers on them so that her corgis didn't slide off the seats into them.

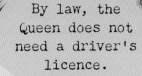

VINTAGE CAR

Prince Charles converted his Aston Martin to run on environmentally friendly biofuel. The fuel is distilled from surplus wine. The car uses the equivalent of 4.5 bottles of wine every 1.5km (1mi)!

CAR? I'D RATHER GO WALKIES.

WANT MORE?

INDEX

NOT-FOR-PARENTS
GREAT BRITAIN
EVERYTHING YOU EVER WANTED TO KNOW

1st Edition
Published September 2012

Conceived by Weldon Owen in partnership with Lonely Planet
Produced by Weldon Owen Publishing
Northburgh House, 10 Northburgh Street
London, EC1V 0AT, UK

weldonowenpublishing.com

Copyright © 2012 Weldon Owen Publishing

WELDON OWEN LTD
Managing Director Sarah Odedina
Publisher Corinne Roberts
Creative Director Sue Burk
Sales Director Laurence Richard
Sales Manager, North America Ellen Towell
Project Editor Shan Wolody
Designer Katy Wall
Design Assistant Haylee Bruce
Index Puddingburn Publishing Services
Production Director Dominic Saraceno
Production Controller Tristan Hanks

Published by

Lonely Planet Publications Pty Ltd ABN 36 005 607 983
90 Maribyrnong St, Footscray, Victoria 3011, Australia

ISBN 978-1-74321-416-9

Printed in China

A WELDON OWEN PRODUCTION

Credits and acknowledgments

Key tcl=top center left; tl=top left; tc=top centre; tcr=top center right;
tr=top right; cl=centre left; c=center; cr=center right; bcl=bottom center
left; bl=bottom left; bc=bottom center; bcr=bottom center right;
br=bottom right; bg=background

Photographs

14tc, 19bc, 22c, 23br, tc, 25bc, tr, 32cl, tcr, 34bcr, 38tr, 39bcr, 43cr, 46-47c,
48cl, 52-53bg, tc, 53tc, 67c, 80c, 81tr, 90cl, tr, 91c **Alamy;** 85tl **Bridgeman
Art Library;** 4cr, 17bc, 18c, cl, 28-29c, 29br, 30cr, 31tl, 34bl, tcr, 35tl, 36bl, cl,
tr, 40-41c, 43tl, 45bc, 52c, 58tc, 60c, 63tcl, 67tl, 69cl, 70cr, 71cl, 72cl, 72-73tc,
73bl, 74-75c, 78c, 80tr, 81bc, 84bcl, 85bc, 87br, tc **Corbis;** 13bl, 14br, 17br,
33bcl, 40br, 43bc, 45c, 73br, 78-79tc, 79bc, cr, tr, 83tr, 94tcr **Dreamstime;**
10-11c, 11cr, tr, 15tl, 19tc, 20c, 21tr, 22bl, 23bc, 25tr, 26cl, 28c, 29tl, 36bc, 37c,
38-39cl, 39tcr, 42c, 44c, 46tc, 47cr, 49cr, tc, 51bcl, br, 56c, 57bc, tr, 58cr, 59cl,
cr, tc, 60tr, 62bc, cl, 63bcr, cr, 64bl, cr, 65tc, 66c, 67tl, 68bl, cr, 70bl, c, tr, 72cr,
74cl, 76cl, cr, 77tc, tcl, 82c, 82-83c, 84bc, 86tr, 88bc, c, 89c, 90cr, 92c, 93tl
Getty Images; 2bc, 3cr, tc, 9c, 10c, cl, 11bc, tc, 12br, 13br, c, 14bc, 15bc, bcr,
c, tcr, tr, 17bcl, bcl, c, c, tc, tcl, 19bl, cr, 20-21tc, 21tcr, 22c, tr, 23c, cl, tcr, 24bc,
25bg, cl, 28br, tr, 29bg, cr, 30cl, tl, 30-31bg, c, 31cr, 32bc, br, tr, 32-33bg,
33bcr, tc, 36cr, tl, 38bc, 40bl, tl, 41bl, tr, 42br, 43cl, tc, tl, 44br, tl, 45cr, tr, 47bc,
c, tc, tr, 48-49c, tc, 49bc, cl, 51cr, tr, 52br, 57cr, tr, 58c, 58-59bl, 59bc, tc, tl,
60tr, 61bg, c, cr, 62-63bg, c, 64-65tr, 65bc, tcr, 66br, 66-67tc, 67cr, 68-69tc,
70bc, br, 71br, tcl, tcr, tr, 72tc, 73cl, tcr, 74-75bg, 75br, cl, tc, 77bc, bcr, c,
78bc, cr, 79bcr, 82bc, bl, 83bl, 84tl, 84-85c, 85br, cl, 86bc, bcr, cl, 87bc, 88bc,
bl, tr, 89r, tl, 90tl, 92-93bc, 93br, c, cl, cr, 94bl, br, br, tc, tr, 95bcl, bcr, bl, tc, tcl,
tcr, tl **iStockphoto.com;** 21bcr, bl **Lonely Planet;** 24cr, tc **Mary Evans
Picture Library;** 9bcr **Northnews;** 2bl, br, 3bc, bl, 8cl, cr, 9bc, tc, tcr, 10bc,
16br, 17cr, 18tr, 20tr, 21c, 29c, 30bc, 31bl, 34c, 35bcr, tcr, 37br, 39tc, 41cr,
43tr, 45bl, br, 46bc, 50c, 51tcl, 52-53bc, 53bcr, cr, 56-57cr, 61bcl, cl, tc, tr, 62cr,
63c, tr, 65bcr, 67bl, 69bcl, bcr, c, cr, tr, 73bc, bcr, 75c, 76bc, bl, c, tr, 77bcl, cr,
79tcr, 82bcl, bcr, tr, 83cr, 84bcr, bcr, cl, tr, 85tcl, 89cl, tl, 94bcl, bcl, 95bc, bc, tr
Shutterstock; 35bc **Topfoto;** 81cl **Wikipedia.**

All repeated image motifs and frames courtesy of **iStockphoto.com**
except 11tr, 29tl, 45tcl, 70tr, 77tc courtesy of **Shutterstock.**

45tcl courtesy of the **University of St Andrews Library**, msCD-14-8.

Illustrations

Cover illustrations by **Chris Corr.**

49c, 85cr **Faz Choudhury/The Art Agency;** 4-5c, 6-7c, 94bc, 95br **Chris
Corr;** 26-27c, 54-55c **Rob Davis/The Art Agency;** 13tc, 16tc **Geri Ford/The
Art Agency.**

All illustrations and maps copyright 2012 Weldon Owen Pty Ltd.

Every effort has been made to trace and contact the copyright holders
prior to publication. If notified, the publisher undertakes to rectify any
errors or omissions at the earliest opportunity.

LONELY PLANET OFFICES

Australia Head Office
Locked Bag 1, Footscray, Victoria 3011
Phone 03 8379 8000 Fax 03 8379 8111

USA
150 Linden St, Oakland, CA 94607
Phone 510 250 6400 Toll free 800 275 8555 Fax 510 893 8572

UK
Media Centre, 201 Wood Lane, London W12 7TQ
Phone 020 8433 1333 Fax 020 8702 0112

lonelyplanet.com/contact